READY FOR
LAUNCH

Me, in the cockpit of an F-14 Tomcat, ready to launch off the deck of the USS *Enterprise*.

READY FOR
LAUNCH

AN ASTRONAUT'S LESSONS
FOR SUCCESS ON EARTH

SCOTT KELLY

CROWN

NEW YORK

All rights reserved. Published in the United States by Crown Books for
Young Readers, an imprint of Random House Children's Books, a division of
Penguin Random House LLC, New York.

Crown and the colophon are registered trademarks
of Penguin Random House LLC.

Photograph credits: 80's Child/Shutterstock.com: i; Sarote Impheng/
Shutterstock.com: 4, 16, 28, 40, 50, 58, 72, 82, 92, 102, 110, 116, 118; Scott Kelly:
ii, 15; NASA: 27, 49, 71 (top and bottom), 90–91, 114–115; NASA/Bill Ingalls:
109; NASA/Robert Markowitz: viii; NASA/Tim Peake: 80–81; NASA/George
Shelton: 57; NASA/Terry Virts: 101; US Navy: 38–39

Visit us on the Web! GetUnderlined.com

Educators and librarians, for a variety of teaching tools,
visit us at RHTeachersLibrarians.com

Library of Congress Cataloging-in-Publication Data
Names: Kelly, Scott, author.
Title: Ready for launch: an astronaut's lessons for success on earth / Scott Kelly.
Description: First edition. | New York: Crown, [2022] | Audience: Ages 12
& up | Audience: Grades 10–12 | Summary: "Using ten life-changing moments
from his path to space, Astronaut Scott Kelly shares his advice for
mastering fear and failure, and turning our daily struggles into rocket
fuel for success"—Provided by publisher.
Identifiers: LCCN 2021040334 (print) | LCCN 2021040335 (ebook) |
ISBN 978-1-5247-6432-6 (hardcover) | ISBN 978-1-5247-6434-0 (ebook)
Subjects: LCSH: Kelly, Scott, 1964–Juvenile literature. |
Success—Juvenile literature. | Conduct of life—Juvenile literature. |
Astronauts—United States—Biography—Juvenile literature.
Classification: LCC TL789.85.K45 A3 2022 (print) |
LCC TL789.85.K45 (ebook) | DDC 629.450092 [B]—dc23

The text of this book is set in 10.5-point Mercury.
Interior design by Ken Crossland

Printed in the United States of America
10 9 8 7 6 5 4 3 2 1
First Edition

To my son Charlie, you've taught me so much.

CONTENTS

INTRODUCTION

––––––

If you told my friends and family when I was a kid in West Orange, New Jersey, that I would grow up to spend 520 days in space, they probably would have laughed. I might have laughed too.

You were more likely to find me climbing a tree…or a house…or a building…than focusing in school.

I'm a former NASA astronaut and probably best known for having spent a year on the International Space Station. During our record-breaking mission, my cosmonaut colleague, Mikhail (Misha) Kornienko; my twin brother, Mark; and I were part of an experiment to better understand the long-term impacts of spaceflight so that other humans might someday be able to make the journey to Mars. I was commander of two different crews over the course of the mission, and it was one of the privileges of my life.

What can you learn from my life in space—both preparing for it on the ground and orbiting Earth at more than 17,000 miles per hour? The answers might surprise you.

I want to share some of the things I've learned that you might not expect—lessons about leadership skills on a dark night on an aircraft carrier in the middle of a churning sea, lessons about the fear you feel with 7 million pounds of engine thrust exploding underneath you, and most of all, lessons about how failure can be a powerful tool to change your life.

There's an idea out there that astronauts are always perfect. "Failure is not an option," right?

That's why I want to take you through some of my life experiences, so you can see why that's just not true. I believe that everyday human failures—if handled correctly—can be one of our greatest opportunities to learn, grow, and succeed.

And I want to show you how.

This book isn't just for people who want to be astronauts—although I do think I have a thing or two to teach about that. I wrote this for anyone who has a dream or a goal but isn't sure they have what it takes to achieve it.

I've had an unusual life. I've been a raw recruit, a fighter pilot, a guinea pig, a cancer survivor, an Instagram trend, a space shuttle and space station commander, a late-night TV show guest, a two-time *New York Times* bestselling author, a husband, and a dad to two amazing kids—and I learned something from all of it.

When I got home to Earth on March 2, 2016, after my year in space, it took me nearly eight months to feel normal again. My vision had changed, and so had my DNA. Some changes still persist…maybe, most of all, the change in my perspective.

My hope is that by the end of this book, your perspective—about yourself, about what's possible, and about your place in the world—will change too.

So let's get started and get ready for launch!

1

FEAR TO TAKE FLIGHT

When I was a kid, I was fearless. I ran with scissors and other sharp objects. I'd climb as high as I could, and then jump right off.

When I was in the eighth grade, my family and I went on a cruise to the Bahamas. We weren't wealthy by any measure, but I think my dad had won some money on a Super Bowl pool...so there we were.

It was the first time I had been out of the country, and the ship was docked at a port in Nassau. I don't remember much about the buffet or onboard entertainment because I was busy jumping off the back of the ship at the challenge of another young guest. Today, that kind of thing goes viral, and not in a positive way. Back then, there was a much smaller audience for my risky behavior. I was lucky to surface in one piece. But I was a slow learner.

It wouldn't be the last time I jumped—or, more accurately, fell—from the back of a ship.

When I was on a port call in Spain aboard a training ship in college, some of my classmates and I hatched a plan to sneak ashore for a night of excitement. We devised a scheme to use a ladder to climb down to the dock. I was the first to go. But the ladder wasn't secured, so I fell about fifty feet directly into the water with a heavy rope-and-wood ladder wrapped around me. Disappearing into the dark waters didn't even faze me at the time. It was just another college prank.

This is the kind of story that you laugh about later, but my casual attitude about falling off large boats was not the quality that showed I had "the right stuff" to be an astronaut. I didn't know it at the time, but that kind of fearlessness was exactly what I would need to overcome if I was going to survive.

My experience of fear started to change when I was in flight school learning to fly the TA-4J Skyhawk, the

US Navy's advanced jet trainer. I remember one particular day at Goliad Field, a little airstrip in the middle of the grasslands of southeast Texas, where I was practicing the skills I'd need to qualify to land on an aircraft carrier. It was uneventful—I did my ten landings and turned around to come home. When I got out of the plane and came up into the ready room, it was clear that something had happened. The other pilots in my class were all looking somber. And quiet.

"What's wrong?" I asked.

Someone told me: "Bryce crashed. He's dead."

Bryce Gearhart was my friend. He had been on the next practice landing session directly after mine. He'd come into his landing pattern a little too fast, yanked back on the stick too hard, pulled too many g's, and lost consciousness. He flew right into the ground.

It had been a pretty routine flight, during the day, in good weather. All of a sudden, my friend—a guy nearly the same age as me—was dead.

I remember thinking, *Life is more fragile than I'd believed.*

In the course of my career in the military and at

NASA, I've lost many friends and colleagues—more than forty people—in aviation and space mishaps. Seeing skilled pilots and astronauts lose their lives has a way of resetting your fear factor. So has nearly killing myself with the smallest mistakes.

One of my near misses happened when I was flying the F-14 Tomcat. It's an impressive machine but challenging to fly, and especially difficult to land on an aircraft carrier.

That night, I was flying combat air patrol in the Persian Gulf with my back seater, Chuck "Gunny" Woodard. We were a couple hundred miles from the ship. It was a perfectly clear night with a bright Moon. The ship signaled that we were allowed to come back early, and we were happy because it was late and we were tired. We had a lot of fuel left, which meant we could get back fast.

I moved the throttles into full afterburner and pretty soon we were supersonic, faster than the speed of sound and heading for the ship. At about thirty miles out, we started our descent. We were supposed to hit that point at 250 knots, but as we approached it, it was clear we were going way too fast. I tried to slow down, pulling too many g's—just like Bryce on the day he crashed.

Then, as we descended, we were suddenly surrounded by a thick fog. Pretty soon the aircraft carrier started turning, which further disoriented me. Suddenly, the radar altimeter started going off, signaling that we were getting close to the water. But with so much going on, the sound was too distracting, so I shut it off.

The next thing I heard was Gunny yelling, "Pull up!"

Instinct kicked in. I pulled back on the stick. When I looked at my instruments, I saw we were passing through 800 feet descending at 4,000 feet per minute. We were only twelve seconds away from hitting the water.

We barely made it. We bottomed out at about 300 feet and then climbed back to our normal altitude. Somehow I was able to put the thoughts of almost being dead behind me and focus on the task at hand: landing on the ship. We managed to regain our composure and flew back to the ship in silence. It wasn't a great landing but good enough considering the circumstances.

That night, I was scared straight. Never again did I

ignore what that radar altimeter was trying to tell me. I depended on that instrument for my life and I always remembered that.

Winston Churchill once said, "Nothing in life is so exhilarating as to be shot at without result."

I have to respectfully disagree. While I've never had to dodge a literal bullet, I do have some experience with nearly killing myself. It's not "exhilarating"; it just scares the crap out of you.

It does, however, have a way of focusing your attention on what matters.

As I advanced in my career and got closer to flying missions in space, I became better acquainted with fear. Feeling it. Respecting it. And knowing exactly how to work through it. But these are skills no one trains you for. To master fear, you have to learn it the hard way.

When the space shuttle was still flying, we used to have a meeting called the "pilot symposium." The space shuttle commanders and pilots—NASA's terms for "pilots" and "copilots"—would gather to go over the most recent landings. We'd review what went right and what went wrong. Every detail was scrutinized...and so was our performance.

At one of these meetings, a commander who'd landed the shuttle recently explained how his leg shook uncontrollably while he was applying the brakes to bring the space shuttle to a stop. As he described this phenomenon, he said he was confused as to why this had happened to his leg.

But all of us who'd spent time on aircraft carriers looked at each other. We realized that the commander was an air force colonel—he'd never had to do the terrifying aircraft carrier landings we had. He hadn't learned this lesson yet.... But we knew exactly what had happened.

What he was describing was completely normal in a high-pressure situation. About half the time I landed on the ship, one of my legs would shake uncontrollably, just as he described. That's what happens when you've got to land a 64-foot-wide fighter jet on a 250-foot-wide landing strip that's often pitching, rolling, heaving, and always moving away from you at an angle. We'd learned the hard way how adrenaline floods your system in high-pressure moments, causing uncontrollable muscle shakes—no matter how well trained you are.

I disagree with FDR's famous line that "the only thing we have to fear is fear itself." In my experience, fear focuses our attention and energy toward the biggest threat and teaches some of life's most valuable lessons.

Fear is in you. It's a part of you. It puts you on high alert. We are biologically wired to experience its effects. And usually, there's a good reason for it. But there's a balance you have to find: you can't let fear overwhelm and incapacitate you, either. If you can master the fear, it will sharply focus your senses and attention and allow you to perform at a higher level of ability.

Prior to my first spaceflight, I was strapped into my seat on the space shuttle several hours before launch, and I had a chance to feel deep, concentrated fear. Lying on my back, atop 4 million pounds of liquid and solid propellants about to be burned by a machine with 2,000 switches and circuit breakers, 230 miles of wiring, and 30,000 fragile tiles that have to withstand temperatures of up to 3,000 degrees, I had time to think about how it would only take one malfunctioning part to cause a catastrophe—not the most reassuring thought in the world.

Especially knowing that the space shuttle *Challenger* blew up shortly after launch, I knew I was taking a risk. The space shuttle had a failure rate of 1.5 percent, a nearly 1 in 70 chance of dying on each mission. Almost the same odds of dying on the beaches of Normandy on D-Day during World War II.

Knowing all this, I thought a lot about my own mortality leading up to each launch. I'd write letters to each of my family members to be opened only in the event of my demise. I gave them to my brother to hold on to. I held on to letters for him on each of his flights, and luckily neither of us ever had the grim job of handing them out.

Every launch I learned to channel my fear into being supremely focused on what I needed to do. I focused on the things I could control and ignored the things I couldn't. By now I had learned that fear wasn't something to brush aside but instead was one of life's greatest teachers and tools.

Often, what's on the other side of fear is what's most rewarding. Change is scary, failure is scary, life can be scary! But if we don't push ourselves and challenge ourselves despite the uncertainty, we will never know what we can achieve. This may be the first time in your life when you have real control over your circumstances and the consequences of your actions. Be thoughtful and consider the repercussions, but take risks and challenge your fears. Apply to that "reach" school or the job you think you might not get. Have outrageous goals and dreams. Embrace fear as your guide. Let it be your call to action. Inaction *guarantees* a disappointing result. So don't let panic paralyze you. Without testing our boundaries and doing the things that most unnerve us, we will never know all that we're capable of and how high we can fly.

Move to achieve big dreams or stand still and stay small.

My failure to land the F-14 on the moving deck of an aircraft carrier almost killed my dream of being an astronaut—and came close to killing me. But mastering that fear and that skill enabled me to move from fighter pilot to test pilot to astronaut.

2

FAILURE IS AN OPTION

I'd love to be less predictable, but there's a decent chance that as you read this, I am watching *Apollo 13*.

I love *Apollo 13*. It's one of those films that I always stop to rewatch if I'm flipping through the channels.

Everybody remembers that moment in the movie when legendary flight director Gene Kranz addresses his Mission Control crew and says, "Failure is not an option."

It's a great scene. Don't get me wrong. But here's some NASA truth for you: Gene didn't actually say that line during the mission. It was later, when a production team was interviewing him for the film and he was asked if people in Mission Control ever panicked. He said, "No.

When bad things happened, we just calmly laid out all the options, and failure was not one of them. We never panicked, and we never gave up on finding a solution."

While it's a great line, I've never gravitated to it as much as other fans seem to. For me, failure has always been an option. I experienced it my whole childhood and sometimes even professionally, and I've never wanted to let go of its lessons.

In fact, when I was a kid, failure was kind of my thing. I couldn't pay attention in class, couldn't do homework, couldn't focus enough to do anything my teachers expected of me. I was the epitome of the late bloomer when it came to learning. My talents lay in other areas, like plummeting from great heights.

When I was in second grade, I still couldn't read well, so my mother took me to see her mother, my grandmother, a special education teacher who specialized in reading. She sat with me patiently, going over letters and sounds, for two or three sessions, until one afternoon when my mother came to pick me up.

As I was leaving, my grandmother finally looked my mother in the eyes and told her, "This kid is just dumb....

He will never learn how to read. I'm not doing this anymore."

It takes a special kind of failure to make your own grandmother resign.

It wasn't that I didn't want to succeed—I always started a new school year with the best of intentions. On the first day I would give myself a stern talking-to: "This is the year I'm going to turn this thing around. This year, I'll pay attention, keep up, do my homework every day, and not be a failure."

And sure enough, by the third day, I'd be three days behind on homework and have no idea what was going on in class. It was hopeless. I would spend the rest of the year staring out the window wondering what was going on outside . . . or staring at the clock to see if it would move any faster. It never did.

Mercifully, I managed to graduate in the bottom half of my high school class and squeaked my way into college. I might not have gone to college at all if I'd been able to think of anything better to do. But once I got there, I vowed to make a fresh start.

By day three, I found myself in a familiar place—three

days behind on homework and having no idea what was going on in class. One more time, my sincere intention had turned into a total failure to engage with the work, which resulted in me just giving up. I couldn't pay attention and had no idea how to study. Eventually I stopped even going to class. Failure seemed like the only option. Success seemed impossible.

Then something happened that changed the entire trajectory of my life.

I was walking across campus and stopped by the bookstore for gum or something (definitely not a book). As I was waiting in line to pay, something caught my eye: a book with a bold title on a graphic cover that captured the feeling of patriotism in forward motion. It beckoned me to pick it up.

It was *The Right Stuff* by Tom Wolfe. I started reading and discovered the passage that explains the title:

"As to just what this ineffable quality was . . . well, it obviously involved bravery. But it was not bravery in that simple sense of being willing to risk your life. The idea seemed to be that any fool could do that, if it was required, just as any fool could throw his life away in the process…"

Something in this book was speaking to me in a way I'd been waiting for.

This was the spark, the inspiration I needed. The characters in Tom Wolfe's book were carrier aviators, then test pilots, then astronauts. But most of all, they were real people. I was sold. I would follow their "flight plan."

It still seems pretty crazy to me that I actually wound up checking off all the items on that to-do list. That I used a 448-page book as a career path. But I did, and it actually all happened—and it worked.

After that, I thought differently about failure.

One thing I've learned is that only when you're willing to risk failure are you aiming high enough. In other words, it's sometimes better to fail at the extraordinary than to succeed at the ordinary.

Being a risk taker is the only way to discover what

your true potential is, who you really are. And if you do that, sure, you might fail along the way... but you might also succeed beyond your wildest dreams.

When I started flying airplanes in the navy, I wasn't especially great at it. The obvious question is: Who had the bad sense to keep letting me fly? At least, that's what I asked myself at times. Maybe the navy had a soft spot for an underdog? Ultimately, I proved that their faith in me wasn't misplaced. But that certainly didn't happen the first time I tried to qualify to land an F-14 Tomcat on an aircraft carrier. In fact, I landed so low on my first attempt that I almost crashed into the back of the ship. The tailhook of the airplane actually hit the stern.

And this was during the day—night landings were going to be much harder. I knew I had screwed up even before my airplane came to a stop. I steadied my nerves and pulled myself together to try again. I taxied forward, preparing to get catapulted off the carrier for my next attempt. But as I followed the directions of the crew on the deck, I soon realized I was being maneuvered into a corner instead of toward the catapult. Then my airplane was being chained down and I was instructed to shut off the engines. This wasn't good.

I jumped out of the airplane and came down the ladder, where the officer who graded our landings immediately confronted me. He gave me a hard, appraising stare, then asked, "Are you sure this career is right for you?" Clearly I wasn't going to land again anytime soon.

I resisted the temptation to defend my actions as he kept talking. He pointed out that I had very nearly crashed—I had noticed that too—but he went on to say I could have killed not just myself but others as well. And that was it. He told me I wasn't going to get another chance. I had disqualified on my first landing attempt.

I was devastated. This was my path to following the trajectory of the guys in *The Right Stuff,* and I might have washed out at Step One.

Over the course of the next week, the commander of the squadron spoke with me about my performance a few times. He said I could learn to fly a heavy cargo plane instead. I wouldn't have to learn to land on the ship. I seriously considered it. It would certainly be easier. And safer.

But I decided I'd rather fail on the harder road than succeed on the easier one.

I wanted to try again. I thought if there was even a chance I could overcome my disastrous first attempt, I should push myself to land on that ship. Only by setting an outrageous goal could I discover what I was capable of achieving.

After a week or so of negotiation with the squadron leadership, I got another shot. Their permission was given with the understanding, however, that I wouldn't be able to just squeak by; I would have to prove that I wasn't dangerous.

To help, the navy teamed me up with a RIO (Radar Intercept Officer) in the back seat, a particular guy who had a reputation for helping troubled carrier pilots like me land on the ship. After practicing for a few sessions, the RIO said to me, "You can fly this airplane okay, but what I realize is that you're too comfortable when things aren't perfect." He recognized that I was not making constant corrections all the time. I was too comfortable with the status quo, and because of that, pretty soon I could find myself off altitude and airspeed, quite possibly leading me to crash into the back of the ship again.

When I returned to the ship to try again, I didn't ace it, but I did well enough to show I wasn't a danger to the ship's crew or myself. I didn't only learn to be a better pilot. I realized that I could never settle for just being comfortable with how things are in life. We must always make small adjustments, or we are going to drift too far off course to correct. But most of all, this experience taught me to never, ever give up.

In the years that followed, I landed successfully many times, both day and night, in fog, torrential downpours, blizzards, gale-force winds, and sandstorms, and not surprisingly, often while scared. As the Tomcat pilots' motto goes, "Anytime, baby."

Failure doesn't have to be a judgment or an ending. For me, it became a challenge, a dare, a measuring stick to prove myself against, and the fuel to push myself further.

Sometimes I come across people who are still stuck in a cycle of failure like I was—wanting to make something of their lives but finding themselves unable to engage with the work and then beating themselves up about it. If that's you, I want to tell you there's a way—you just need to find a spark of inspiration that drives you forward and makes the impossible possible.

Failure is not only always an option but also a necessity in life. If you are not failing, you are not living. It is through failure that we learn. It is through failure that we gain experience, grow, and build the resilience needed to succeed.

While the *Challenger* explosion was one of NASA's worst tragedies, the risk and challenge of spaceflight only made it more appealing to me.

3

ENDEAVOR TO LEAD

Maybe at some schools, students are taught about leadership in a required course, but that course was never offered at any school I attended. I wish it had been.

When I was younger, leadership was something we talked about without anyone ever trying to explain it. The navy ROTC offered a course called Leadership, but it was more about the history of leaders, not a how-to course. But you have leadership opportunities all around you, on sports teams, in student government, during group projects—really, any organized activity—and knowing how to lead will help you achieve now and in the future.

For me, learning to lead was a process of trial and

error—noticing what worked and what didn't. I also watched the leaders I served under throughout my career, both good and bad. I learned a lot from the good ones, and maybe just as much from the bad ones.

One of the first opportunities I had to truly lead was at SUNY Maritime College, a military-style school that trains officers for the merchant marines, the US Navy, USMC, and the coast guard. In my third year, I was chosen to be the chief indoctrination officer. I'd be leading a group of twenty of my classmates, overseeing the training of the entire freshman class.

In my own freshman year, the school's military-style training really worked for me. The structure and discipline was something I craved, including having a drill-sergeant type literally screaming in my face.

So I figured I should bring the same style to my new leadership position. They yelled, so I yelled—I yelled at the freshmen I was overseeing. I yelled to push them past their limits. I yelled when they fell short and yelled when they did a good job. I yelled myself hoarse, and then yelled some more.

And I thought all that yelling was working. I saw the

cadets under me improve, including a few tough cases—other screwups like myself—so I patted myself on the back. I was being a good leader and role model! I thought I was being tough when necessary but also understanding and compassionate when needed.

That was at the start of the year. By the end, it was clear not everyone agreed.

As we prepared for a summer at sea, I started receiving a series of angry anonymous letters. The letters warned me not to stand too close to the railing with my back turned. The writer made it clear that he'd like nothing better than to see me thrown overboard. He was one of my cadets and he hated me.

I was stunned. How could one of the cadets feel that way about their leader? How could one of my cadets feel that way about *me*? Did I need to be looking over my shoulder?

When I was younger, there was a belief that the tough approach was always most effective, and while that was true for me as a kid who couldn't do his homework or follow through on anything, I now think I should have stopped to consider each cadet's situation rather than applying the same approach to everyone. Good leaders adjust to do what works best for each particular situation or person. We are all unique, so different styles of leadership speak to us in different ways. In retrospect, instead of yelling at everyone, I should have been more thoughtful and adjusted my style to what worked for each person I was trying to lead instead of just applying what had worked for me.

I should have been less George Patton and more George Washington.

Receiving that threatening letter changed me. It woke me up to the fact that you can hold people to high standards—you can even admonish them when necessary—but you also have to let them know that they matter, they are important, and they are respected. I still wanted to have high expectations for people I was leading, but first I had to have higher expectations for myself. This was my first real lesson in leadership.

My next big lesson came a few years later, when I was flying the F-14 Tomcat in a US Navy fighter squadron.

Our commanding officer, or CO, was the stereotypical fighter pilot you see in movies—arrogant, cocky, and full of himself—but without the talent to back it up. He talked the talk but couldn't walk the walk, as they say.

Fighter pilots often joke that a full Moon is called a "commander's Moon" because that's when the squadron commanders want to fly. Landing on an aircraft carrier in the dark can be absolutely terrifying because when the horizon isn't visible, pilots feel like they're flying upside down, even when they're not. The more senior pilots get to choose when to fly, so of course they pick the nights with a bright Moon—a commander's Moon.

But this one particular night it was really, really dark. With no Moon, there was no horizon visible. Would our commander fly? He was slated to go and was getting ready. He preflighted the jet, checking to make sure it was safe, and when he was done, he told the maintenance department the airplane was "down." Not safe to fly. He claimed it had a "loose-fitting canopy gas line," which, if it were true, could be dangerous because it's part of the ejection system.

The squadron's maintenance chief disagreed, so

he started arguing with them—an argument he won, of course, because he was the squadron commanding officer.

But still, our CO couldn't just skip flying that sortie without it affecting his flight rate numbers—that would reflect badly on his leadership as squadron commander, and he had his eyes on becoming an admiral someday. So that meant he had to get some other poor sucker to go out on this dark night, and that poor sucker was me.

Our CO told me about the issue with the canopy fitting. It was unsafe for *him,* but now that it was my turn to fly, he claimed it had been fixed—amazing! So now it was safe for me to fly on this darkest of nights. He even did this weird demonstration using a red Bic pen—he held it out to me and had me pull on the cap.

He said, "See, this is how much force it should take to pull out the canopy fitting." I pulled on the cap of the pen, confused. I had no idea what a pen cap had to do with an F-14.

But he was in command, so I acted like it made sense. I headed through the red-lit passageways, up to the pitch-black flight deck. It took my eyes a while to adjust.

It was a level of darkness that I had never really seen be-fore. I preflighted the Tomcat, checked that it was ready to go, including the canopy fitting. I pulled on the canopy fitting just like he instructed, and it seemed to require a similar amount of force to dislodge as the cap of the Bic pen. But it also seemed ridiculous. This was not some-thing we'd normally check.

I climbed down the ladder to talk to the senior chief petty officer in charge of flight deck operations. He asked, "You good to go, sir?"

I told him I was and asked what they did to fix the airplane. He admitted they didn't do anything. We both knew, without saying it, that our CO had been, well, not truthful. He wasted everyone's time with a fake problem, because even though there was nothing to fix, they had to investigate, troubleshoot, do the paperwork, make be-lieve they actually repaired the equipment, etc.—just so he could get out of doing a tough job, setting a poor ex-ample as our leader.

So I launched into one of those deep black nights that haunt the dreams of carrier aviators, knowing the land-ing was guaranteed to be terrifying.

I felt then, and I still feel now, that our CO shouldn't have sent any of us into conditions that he wasn't willing to fly in himself. Good leaders hold themselves to higher standards than they demand from those they lead. Our CO was not that kind of leader. That's where I learned the term DAISNAID: "Do As I Say, Not As I Do." Our commanding officer was a DAISNAID leader—we actually called him that behind his back—and I was determined never to be one myself.

There are many different leadership styles, but after the jolt of receiving that threatening letter at SUNY Maritime, I stopped locking into just one particular style. I let the situation determine which leadership style would work best for me.

Oftentimes I found myself being the "servant" type of leader, making sure I gave my people the skills and resources they needed to do the job. Sometimes a good leader follows the principle of democracy. What do the majority of people want to do? On these occasions when I had to make a decision in space, I'd simply ask my crew to vote, to make them feel included and respected.

In rare situations, like when there's a fire on the

space station, the "autocrat" would be the most effective type of leader, deciding what to do in a crisis and announcing the plan quickly. If a fire alarm is blaring on the space station, or if we are venting air out into space, there needs to be one person who states clearly what everyone's going to do, and that's the commander. But applying that leadership style every day, in every situation, is both damaging and limiting.

This adaptable style of leadership is often referred to as situational leadership, and it has worked best for me. It's flexible, allowing you to take stock of your team members, weigh all the variables of your work environment, and choose the leadership style that best meets the goals and situation at hand. Be fluid. Team needs and goals change. Adapt accordingly.

As a leader, I never wanted my crewmates to follow *me*. I wanted them to follow principles I believed in and tried to model, like empathy, integrity, accountability, honesty, and courage.

Lead like a partner, not like a boss.

Flying with my Radar Intercept Officer (RIO) Bill "Smoke" Mnich helped me fine-tune the skills I needed as a test pilot, and our successful partnership helped me become a strong leader.

4

FLYING BY HEART

I'd been learning to land aircraft in challenging circumstances for most of my navy career. But once I got to NASA, I had a steeper learning curve ahead of me, because landing the space shuttle is the hardest thing a pilot can do. But even more than the technical skills I had to master, I had to learn another important trait all leaders must have—heart.

Early on, before I had been assigned to a mission, I was training to fly the space shuttle. A lot of that training has to do with learning to land. The shuttle came in at an incredibly steep angle, ten times steeper than an airliner. And it didn't have engines like an airplane. The shuttle was basically a heavy glider with the aerodynamics of a brick. At NASA we called it a flying soda machine. The stakes were always high because we only had one chance to get our landing right. To practice, we'd use the Shuttle Training Aircraft, a jet that was altered to simulate the drag of the space shuttle.

One day during a break in training, I was sitting at a desk checking my email when a senior astronaut, Curt Brown, came up behind me and tapped me on the shoulder. When I turned to look at him, he just said, "You. Come with me."

I followed Curt into an office, where he closed the door and looked right in my eyes. Had I messed up? Was I being pulled out of training? It didn't look good, whatever it was. I felt like I had done something wrong.

He poked me in the chest with his finger and said, "You'd better have it together, because we're flying in space in six months."

What? Had I just been assigned to my first flight?

Now, this is usually a once-in-a-lifetime moment for an astronaut, one of the highlights of any NASA career. Usually this is a less aggressive, more positive event that starts with being called into the chief astronaut's office in Houston and ends with congratulations, handshakes, and maybe a drink at The Outpost later in the day.

Not when dealing with Curt, though. I had just been chosen for an important mission to repair the Hubble Space Telescope. And I was the first American astronaut in my class to be assigned to a flight. Yet he was aggressively poking me in a tiny room with knotty pine paneling and a buzzing fluorescent light. I sensed this important moment could have gone better.

But Curt was going to be the leader of our mission, and I would learn a lot from him—lessons both positive and negative.

Early in our training, Curt got in a heated discussion with one of our crewmates about something related to our mission. When the other guy left the room, Curt said to me, "Man, that Goody Two-shoes really pisses me off."

Maybe he was trying to ease some tension or make me feel included since I was the only rookie on the crew—I think a lot of new leaders try to do this—but it was the opposite of good team-building. It wasn't the best start to our training, especially on one of my first days with the crew.

As we got further into training, I learned that Curt was incredibly competent with every technical aspect of his job—perhaps the best ever—and given that the space shuttle is the most complex machine ever built, that's saying something. But as time went on I came to realize no amount of technical skill can make up for the "soft skills" that are so crucial to leading a successful team.

We were training for our mission using a simulator—a mock-up of the shuttle's flight deck designed to throw us around a bit—to mimic the motion we would experience on a real flight. Like the Epcot space ride only with fewer screaming children. As we got closer to the launch date, we'd even dress in our full launch and entry space-suits to prepare for the real thing.

On one of those days, we were in the middle of a complex scenario. Curt was buried in the left side of the cockpit working some complex cooling system problem, while at the same time the control center in Houston called up for us to change the communication channel on one of the computers—a task that would normally also be Curt's.

Because he was so busy, I thought I would help out

and change the port mode for him. I typed the command into the keypad, pressed execute, and moved on with my next task, feeling good about helping my commander.

When Curt had finally resolved the cooling system problem, he suddenly realized that one of the computers was now communicating on a different channel than it had been earlier. "What happened to the FF1 MDM?" he asked.

"I port moded it," I said. "You were so busy, I figured I'd help out."

Curt turned sideways in his seat and looked me in the eye. Then he pulled his arm back as far as he could, made a fist, and punched me. Not an easy thing to do while wearing a full pressure suit and strapped into his seat in a five-point harness...so this was clearly intentional.

"Never do that again!" he barked.

"Yes, sir" was all I said.

I'm pretty thick-skinned and was able to shake off the dressing-down, but I think a lot of people would be thrown off by this behavior.

I understood that Curt needed to make his message clear. If I'd kept monkeying around with his controls while his back was turned, it might have caused serious problems, possibly even getting us killed. He needed to get my attention clearly and memorably, and I have to admit I've never forgotten it. Kind of like when my grandmother fired me from reading lessons.

In Curt's defense, he had flown five space shuttle missions in six years. That's an unbelievable pace—some astronauts fly only one or two missions over their entire careers—so I can imagine that gearing up for a sixth flight may have really worn out the limits of his patience for rookies. It probably would have worn me out too.

Curt and I are still friends. I learned a great deal from him about how to be an astronaut and how to command a space shuttle flight . . . but his approach lacked one of the most important traits a leader can have: empathy.

In March 2015, I launched into space on a Russian Soyuz spacecraft from the Baikonur Cosmodrome in Kazakhstan for my last mission. I flew with a Russian cosmonaut named Gennady Padalka. Gennady holds the record for the most time in space: 879 days. That's almost two and a half years. And it's 878 days and 22 hours longer than Yuri Gagarin, the first person in space, spent off planet. We spent six months of my nearly yearlong mission together.

Gennady was incredibly good at the technical aspects of his job, but he also had great people skills. For 154 days, he would float down from the Russian Service Module to the US segment, where we would be starting our work for the day. He'd hang out in the vestibule and just chat with us for ten or fifteen minutes. What are you working on? How is your family back on Earth? Sleeping okay? Those kind of things.

There wasn't a lot of mission-critical information exchanged in these little meetings. But by taking the time to talk with us, Gennady was letting us know that each of us mattered to him—not just as a crewmate or coworker but as a person. He cared how we were feeling, how we were handling the stresses of living in space. He cared about our families. He wanted to be involved in our lives and to help us in any way he could, even when it wasn't his job.

I learned from Gennady how important it is to let people know that they matter to you. I took that lesson with me when I became the commander of the space station. Every morning, I would make the time to float over to the Russian segment and catch up with the cosmonauts, and even though it looked like we were just chatting, I knew this was time well spent.

Empathy is one of those soft skills that's hard to teach, but that I've come to learn is at the core of good leadership. It builds relationships, allows you to see the root of a problem, and lets everyone feel like they can be honest about their mistakes so they can improve.

Empathy is not just how you lead; it's how you build new generations of thoughtful leaders. It's a crucial ingredient to every successful team effort. And take it from me: it's a lot more effective than a punch in the arm.

Our Friday night group dinners helped bring us together as a crew and were a great example of the many ways when Gennady's empathetic leadership style shined. Front row: Kimiya Yui (Japan) and Sergey Volkov (Russia); second row: Aidyn Aimbetov (Russia), Mikhail (Misha) Kornienko (Russia), Gennady Padalka (Russia), and me; third row: Andreas Mogensen (Denmark) and Kjell Lindgren (US).

5

___

COMMANDING DECISIONS

There are no routine days in space. One day you'll get a call from a third-grade class that wants to hear about how we go to the bathroom in zero gravity. Another day, you might get a call from Mission Control saying that, thanks to a baseball-sized hole in the heat shield, you might burn up on reentry.

I got that terrible call a day or so into commanding my first space shuttle mission. The heat shield on the underside of *Endeavour* had a hole in it. A similar issue had killed seven of my colleagues on the shuttle *Columbia* a few years earlier.

There was a lot of discussion about what we should do to address the issue. We could do a spacewalk to try to repair the heat shield, but spacewalks are extremely risky on their own and there was always a danger we would just damage the heat shield more while trying to fix it. If we left the hole as it was, though, the heat of re-entry might tear the space shuttle apart.

As commander, I had a lot of say in what our approach was going to be. It would have been tempting to make a quick decision on my own, but over the years I've spent leading and following, I've learned that the best decisions aren't made that way.

Instead, I decided to take each crew member aside, one by one, in private. I kept a picture of the heat shield damage and a printout of some analysis from the ground in my back pocket so I'd be able to ask each crew member individually for their honest opinion.

I took this to such an extreme that I asked everyone I could—I even asked the astronaut and Russian cosmonauts who weren't coming back with us on the shuttle.

Why not call a meeting? Why not make a decision together as a group? Well, I've seen what can happen when people try to make decisions in groups—one person will offer an opinion, and if that person is knowledgeable or

52

well-respected, everyone else may go along with what they said. Groupthink sets in. People aren't even conscious of doing this sometimes—it's something we do as a social species to get along, and it's often a useful instinct. But in a case like this, it could be deadly.

There is a room in Mission Control in Houston, Texas, that's used for serious meetings and making important decisions. We call it "the Sports Bar" because it has a bunch of TVs on the walls like someplace you'd spend an NFL Sunday. There is a sign on one of those walls that says, NONE OF US IS AS DUMB AS ALL OF US. Of course, the opposite can be true sometimes too, and collaboration and working as a team can be valuable. But the lemmings-going-over-a-cliff groupthink contributed to both the *Challenger* and *Columbia* disasters.

Ultimately, with the input of my crew, thorough analysis, and the advice of flight controllers and leadership on the ground, we decided that the hole in the heat shield posed less of a risk than attempting a repair.

We fired the deorbit engines and as we came out of darkness and started hitting the atmosphere, the fire outside the space shuttle continued to build. Pretty soon we were in a 3,000-degree fireball, falling toward Earth at an incredible speed. Our entire crew was mostly silent as *Endeavour* approached the point where *Columbia* had come apart. As we transitioned through that altitude, my pilot, Scorch, said, "Passing through peak heating."

"Understand," I replied. I let about twenty seconds go by, then added, "Looks like we dodged that bullet," as we all reflected on the loss of our seven colleagues four and a half years prior and our gratitude for not suffering a similar fate. Thirty minutes later, we landed safely at the Kennedy Space Center.

But this kind of collaborative decision-making can help in other places too—like a Level I Trauma Center in Tucson, Arizona.

Gabrielle Giffords, my twin brother Mark's wife, was a US congresswoman when I flew my third spaceflight, a long-duration mission on the ISS. On January 8, 2011, I was halfway through that six-month mission when I received the shocking news that a gunman had tried to assassinate Gabby at an event she called "Congress on Your Corner," shooting her and twelve others, and killing six people—including a nine-year-old girl named Christina-Taylor Green. At one point the news media incorrectly reported that Gabby had died. Her injuries were horrific and considered by most to be un-survivable. My brother, Mark, was constantly having to make difficult decisions about her care. He found himself in meetings with many of her caretakers—trauma surgeons, brain surgeons, neurologists. But instead of just hearing out the top doctor in charge, Mark would go a step further. He would find one quiet person in the back of the room and ask them who they were.

"I'm just an intern," they might say or, "I'm just a nurse."

But Mark didn't care what the person's training was. "What do you think?" he would ask. "What are we missing? What are we overlooking?" Even if they hadn't been in the room long, their opinion mattered and he learned valuable information by gathering as many perspectives as he could.

I learned as much from hearing how he handled Gabby's care as I did from anyone I flew with in space.

The smartest person in the room is usually the person who knows how to tap into the intelligence of *every* person in the room.

We all make hundreds of decisions every day. Some decisions are minor, like whether to eat breakfast or not. Other decisions, however, are about opportunities that can change your life, like whether to go away to college or commute from home or whether to take a paying summer job, an internship, or a volunteer opportunity. Each decision is a fork in the road. You are not a mere passenger in life; you are the commander.

When you have taken control of your decisions, make sure to learn from what worked or what didn't. We do this in the military and at NASA. It's called the debrief and is considered a critical part of the process because it will help hone your decision-making skills for handling future problems and will help you learn from your successes and failures.

Behind every successful leader is a constellation of difficult decisions made.

Landing *Endeavour* safely was a satisfying ending to a potentially deadly mission.

6

DIVERSITY IS A FORCE MULTIPLIER

I showed up at the Johnson Space Center in August 1996 with forty-three other brand-new astronaut candidates. We were the largest class ever recruited, and the other astronauts called us "the Sardines." At first I didn't understand why, until one day when all forty-four of us had to move from our offices to another building for a meeting.

As we all tried to cram into elevators, I saw how the nickname made sense. Twenty people standing in an elevator made for fifteen. Not only was this designed to move us from one floor to another, we joked that it was a test to see whether we had claustrophobia. (We were all tested for claustrophobia during astronaut selection by being zipped into a thick rubber bag for an undetermined length of time while wearing a heart monitor.) Had that elevator malfunctioned, we may have lost a few candidates and would have had to change our name to "the Minnows."

But in addition to being big, our class was very diverse. The first few astronaut classes had been all white men, but starting in 1978, women and people of color had been included in every class and have been flying together in space ever since.

Our class had nine international astronauts representing seven different countries and nine women, three of whom were Black. This was by far the most diverse group of people I had ever worked with, coming from a background in military aviation that was exclusively male, overwhelmingly white, and predominantly middle-class. (As an example of how slow the military aviation community is to change, the navy only graduated its first Black woman tactical jet pilot in the summer of 2020.)

For the next two years, the forty-four of us did intensive coursework in aeronautical engineering, orbital mechanics, Earth and planetary science, and space shuttle systems training. Those of us who would be actually piloting the space shuttle spent a great deal of time learning its complex, interconnected systems and how to land it safely.

While the pilots worked to master those skills, mission specialists trained to conduct spacewalks safely in a giant swimming pool called the Neutral Buoyancy Laboratory, the largest indoor pool in the world at nearly forty feet deep with full-scale exterior mock-ups of the space shuttle and the ISS.

But our training didn't stop there. We also had to go through diversity training. There was a fair amount of quiet grumbling about this, as I've heard there is at other kinds of workplaces. I think my classmates by and large, including me, felt like they didn't need to take time out of a busy work schedule to talk about inclusiveness and how to get along.

I had spent my life up to that point in pretty homogenous settings. My fighter squadron, VF-143—the World Famous Pukin' Dogs—was a great bunch of guys but seriously lacked diversity. Before that, both my military-style college and my hometown of West Orange, New Jersey, were overwhelmingly white at the time. My high school class was a mix of Jewish, Irish, and Italian American kids with only a handful of students who weren't white.

Knowing I didn't have much experience working with women or anyone from backgrounds different from my own, and since I didn't have much choice in attending the training, I figured I might as well pay attention. In one class we were talking about cultural differences and the instructor brought up the fact that many Americans think Europeans smell. I turned to my French astronaut colleague sitting next to me, Philippe Perrin, and whispered, "How does that make you feel, him saying that you smell?"

Philippe whispered back, "He didn't say we smell bad. We smell like people. You Americans smell like soap."

I realized he was right—what counts as smelling "bad" depends on what you're used to.

This was a small moment, but I was starting to absorb

the lesson here: it's all about your perspective, and just because my own perspective as a middle-class straight white cis man is reflected all around me doesn't mean it's the only one or the best one for every situation.

I'm grateful that throughout my twenty years at NASA, I had the chance to work with a variety of people from different backgrounds. I flew in space with a French engineer, a schoolteacher from Idaho, a Swiss astrophysicist, a Welsh Canadian doctor, a Black American test pilot, the first Italian woman fighter pilot, a Japanese test pilot, a Kazakh fighter pilot, a Danish engineer, and more Russian cosmonauts than I can count. And of course mostly white dudes like myself. We all spoke different languages, believed different things, problem-solved in different ways—and we all got the job done.

Diverse people bring different strengths to a team, and when you're trying to do something as challenging as flying in space, you need as many different strengths as you can get.

When I was preparing for my first long-duration spaceflight, I was slated to overlap for a majority of the

159 days with Cady Coleman. Cady was a military officer in the air force, and she was the veteran of two space shuttle missions, just like me.

But Cady and I were as different as two military officers could be. So when Cady first arrived on the ISS, I could see why people had been worried. For months, we would have to cooperate and live together in an area the size of the inside of a 747 crammed full of stuff. Some of our colleagues were seriously concerned that Cady and I wouldn't be able to get along (or that we might kill each other).

Cady didn't entirely live her life by schedules, and I would often find her in the little window-filled module called the Cupola, looking out at Earth and playing her flute at three in the morning. Throughout the workday, I always knew what Cady was working on because she would leave experiments and projects half-done, to be finished up later, or there would be scraps and remnants of her activities just…floating around.

But whatever else she needed to do, Cady always made time to speak with people on the ground, especially schoolchildren, even beyond the many events

NASA scheduled for us. She made time for art and music, even playing the first Earth-space duet on her flute with the founder of the band Jethro Tull.

Unlike Cady, I had always seen the public-relations part of my job as a nuisance. I knew it needed to be done because the public has a right to know how their tax dollars are being spent and to feel involved in the space program. After all, they are paying for it and their interest and support is critical to its success. But I'm not a newscaster or a YouTuber, and I didn't really enjoy being pressed into service as one.

I felt that my job was to command the space station, to carry out the many complex procedures and experiments I was tasked with, to run a tight ship, to keep my crew safe, and, you know, to keep the aging ISS from falling apart. Which seemed like plenty. I didn't see the point of making cute videos, taking on extra interviews and speeches, or generally engaging the public the way Cady did.

One day, the crew had to take part in a standard public-affairs interview. I answered the questions in my factual, straightforward "are-we-done-yet" tone, anxious to get it over with and on to the more serious work we had planned for the day.

This was very clearly not my favorite part of the day. Later, Cady confronted me. She said, "You know, if you don't sound excited about what we're doing up here, no one else will be, either."

She was right. Just because it made me uncomfortable to be on camera didn't mean it wasn't an important part of my job. I needed to learn to do it better, and Cady was the perfect teacher. Just watching Cady was instructive, and by the time I flew a yearlong mission on the space station, four years later, you could hear the difference.

Around this time, with the help of my wife, Amiko, who was a NASA public affairs officer, I'd also figured out Twitter and Instagram. We'd been building up the YearInSpace hashtag. I did a Reddit Ask Me Anything. I showed off the first flower we grew in space. I played water Ping-Pong and had a Super Bowl party for one. I juggled fruit, which is still impressive even though the fruit just kind of hangs there in microgravity. I also explained how I had to clean up a gallon-sized ball of urine and acid. I explained that space smells like burning metal. And that my favorite David Bowie song is not "Space Oddity" but probably "Under Pressure."

It wasn't what I thought I'd been training for, but this sort of work was able to bring all kinds of people into the experience of our mission and bring them closer to science, engineering, and the amazing things we accomplish when we all work together.

It was Cady—with her flute and her positive attitude—who made that possible. I've flown in space with forty different people, and I learned something from all of them (even those I wasn't particularly fond of). I hope they learned something from me. Sometimes they showed me very positive things, like on my first flight when my crewmate Jean-François Clervoy taught me to experience the mission through the wondering eyes of a child. But sometimes you can learn from other people's mistakes and shortcomings, like when two cosmonauts put their personal animosity toward one another ahead of the mission, or when an American astronaut was such a self-victimizing complainer that I was ordered to counsel him upon my arrival to ISS.

In training to fly on a Russian spacecraft, I've spent a lot of time in Russia, getting to know the culture and learning to speak the language (not very well, I might add). I've had the chance to get to know Russian literature and history in a way I never expected. And it all made me a better astronaut and a better person.

Even though we work so closely together on the space program, there's always potential for conflict and challenges, particularly with the Russians. Our two countries are not always the friendliest. I guess you could call us frenemies.

But once we're in space we set all that aside, because we rely on cosmonauts and they rely on us. Even when our countries are adversaries, we can work together toward a shared goal that has mutual benefits. Space is a great place to do that, because no one owns it. It's common ground where peaceful scientific collaboration can occur.

I've learned from my colleagues who grew up in different cultures, practice different religions, and were born with different sexual orientations. It's only recently that NASA has recruited astronauts who openly acknowledge a same-sex partner, and I hope to see a transgender astronaut in my lifetime. I have a transgender son who is one of the smartest and kindest people I have ever had the privilege of knowing, and it would be a loss to NASA if they didn't include people like him among their ranks someday.

In retrospect, I think the people who warned that Cady and I would kill each other in space underestimated both of us and overlooked the power of our differences. I try to keep this in mind when I see people who seem very different working together, and I want to encourage them to see their differences as strengths—what we referred to in the military as a "force multiplier," a tool that helps you expand your effectiveness. Think of how you use a hammer to drive in a nail. You can use the same amount of energy hitting that nail with the palm of your hand, but that will never be as effective as when you use a hammer. The hammer is a force multiplier, just as working with people who are different from you adds power to your team.

Cady and I are now friends for life. And when she thinks of the mission we flew together, I hope she remembers as fondly as I do the times I'd find her playing her flute in the Cupola and I couldn't help but tell her, "Cady, go to sleep! It's a school night. You know who's in bed already? Jethro Tull."

Diversity casts a wider net in the search for talent, skills, and experience, and comes up the richer for it. Our differences become our strengths when we allow ourselves to learn from each other.

TOP: The Mercury 7, NASA's first astronauts, were also top military pilots but not a diverse bunch.

BOTTOM: But my very diverse astronaut class was composed of nine women and thirty-five men: thirty-five Americans, including three African Americans and one Japanese American; two Japanese; two Canadians; and five Europeans.

7

BLAME ME

We've all known people who take credit for things they didn't do. But, you know, they're somehow never to blame when things go wrong. While I don't think failure should reflect badly on us—because being flawless means we're not challenging ourselves enough—I do think we need to own up to our failures.

People who dodge blame seem to think that by hiding their failures, they can convince everyone they're perfect—but I believe the opposite is true. People who can accept blame squarely, take responsibility, and move on come across as stronger and more trustworthy than people who never accept fault.

I've believed this for a long time, but I had a chance to

prove it during my year in space. About eight months in, we were preparing for the arrival of a Russian resupply vehicle. The resupply vehicles bring us everything from fuel to water and food to spare parts and equipment for experiments. They even sent me a gorilla suit, a joke gift from my brother. But before this next shipment could arrive, various pieces of equipment on the exterior of the ISS needed to be locked into place.

One of the items was a cart that had been designed to transport equipment along the truss, the structure that holds the giant gold solar arrays in place. This cart had never quite worked the way it was intended to, and today it had gotten stuck and stopped responding when Houston tried to move it. The Russian space agency told NASA they were going to dock the resupply spacecraft regardless of whether our equipment was locked down properly.

This was against NASA's wishes and flight rules. It was the kind of situation that had the potential to spark an international incident in space. The lead flight director, Emily Nelson, called up to explain the situation to me. We started to discuss what could have caused this cart to become stuck, and Emily mentioned the possibility that at some point in the past, an astronaut had accidentally locked the cart's brakes while doing a spacewalk.

I had done a spacewalk just a few weeks earlier. Her words stung because I'd been working in exactly that area.

"I think I know who screwed that up," I responded. "I'm responsible."

There was a pause on the other end of the connection. "How certain are you?" Emily asked.

"Very certain," I said.

Emily seemed surprised that I was actually volunteering to take the blame. There had been dozens of spacewalks carried out to repair hundreds of components on the space station over the fifteen years it had been inhabited, and other astronauts had had their hands on that cart in the recent past.

If I'd just kept my mouth shut, the locked brake on that cart would have wound up being one of those things that was nobody's fault. But I didn't think that was the right thing to do. Failing to speak up would have wasted time and just delayed fixing the problem.

So, a few days later, I suited up for an emergency spacewalk to fix the cart. A spacewalk—even under normal circumstances—is incredibly challenging, time-consuming, and risky. But when you are cutting corners to do it quickly, it is even more dangerous.

Together with Tim Kopra, my NASA astronaut colleague who had recently arrived on the space station, I went outside and made my way from the space station's air lock, moving hand-over-hand out on the truss to where the cart was located. I mashed the brake release with my gloved hand, freeing the cart and probably exclaiming something to the effect of "Some dumbass locked that thing."

The spacewalk was successful, and the Russian vehicle was able to dock without incident.

Going outside to work in the vacuum of space had been the most challenging thing I'd ever done up to that point, and I wasn't especially looking for a reason to do it again. But it was important to me to own up to my mistake and do what I could to fix it.

Sometimes people are rewarded when they dodge blame or even cover up their mistakes, and I've seen this in action as well. The Russian space agency has a very different way of managing and paying their cosmonauts than NASA does its astronauts, and part of that has to do with how blame is assigned.

Both astronauts and cosmonauts are paid extra when they are flying in space. In the case of the cosmonauts, they get a significant bonus of somewhere between 350 to 700 US dollars per day, depending on how experienced they are. So for someone like my friend Gennady who has spent 879 days in space, that can really add up.

By contrast, American astronauts only receive an additional five dollars a day, the US government rate of per diem when everything is provided—food, shelter, etc. But our salaries are much higher to begin with, which means we are less dependent on that bonus to make ends meet than the cosmonauts are, which is where the problem comes in.

Cosmonauts are given higher bonuses for their achievements—like a successful spacewalk. But every time they make a "mistake," their bonuses are lowered. A cosmonaut can lose their daily bonus for flipping the wrong switch, missing a step in an experiment, or making similar everyday human errors. There's actually a person in Russian Mission Control whose only job is to track the mistakes of cosmonauts. And when each cosmonaut comes back to Earth, they have to sit in a room with the mistake tracker and an accountant to argue over each success and each mistake to determine what their bonus is going to be.

I experienced firsthand the way this sort of negotiation is supposed to work when I was preparing to fly on the Russian Soyuz spacecraft. I learned that it was part of the ritual to argue over every single error. It took me a while to understand that we were actually expected to create elaborate excuses about how we hadn't done anything wrong, how everything was somebody else's fault, and that no blame should be attached to us. I came to think of this practice as "blame-smithing," and some people were quite skilled at it. I never took to blame-smithing, and I think it annoyed the Russians that when it was my turn to make an impassioned speech about how I didn't flip the wrong switch, I'd just say, "Yep, that was me."

Once training was over and we were in space, the

question of blame got real for my Russian friends. They were always dealing with the possibility of losing money for the smallest mistakes, so I'd tell them to blame me. "Just say the American did it."

As far as I could see, it was a win-win. They wouldn't lose their bonus and their control center wouldn't spend a day trying to figure out what really went wrong because their cosmonauts were avoiding responsibility. Being honest that an error was made, even at my expense, was just a better use of everyone's time and resources.

Real teamwork means it's crucial for everyone to admit their mistakes. If you want to solve problems, move fast, and make sure everyone's doing their best, you can't punish people for speaking up. That's true in space, but it applies anytime, anywhere.

It's so much better to just be honest and move on. But if you get in a bind, you're welcome to say, "The American did it."

Taking responsibility for a mistake I made during a spacewalk was the right thing to do, and was much easier for an American astronaut to admit than it would have been for a Russian cosmonaut, due to differences in our organizations' cultures.

8

SOMETIMES IT *IS* ROCKET SCIENCE

In my twenty years at NASA, one thing that became abundantly clear is that not everything we did was rocket science. But sometimes the problems astronauts face *are* literally rocket science, and when they are, we need to listen to the rocket scientists.

The importance of this weighs on me every day. In recent years, I've become increasingly troubled by a general move toward distrusting experts. Instead, people are listening to social media, untrusted sources, or public figures who claim to have "very good brains." Conspiracy theories seem to be spreading more widely than they used to, and the effects on our society could be disastrous.

Scientists tell us that climate change is real, that

vaccines work, and that Earth is round—these things are not up for debate, and it disturbs me that so many people seem to think they are.

I was once giving a talk at the Hayden Planetarium in New York with astrophysicist Neil deGrasse Tyson, and during the question-and-answer period, a man stood up to ask a question. As he talked, it became clear that he had come to the event to try to confront me.

This guy, in particular, had come to the planetarium just to ask me to explain why he could see tiny bubbles in some footage of one of my spacewalks from the ISS.

At first, I didn't even understand the question. "Bubbles?" I repeated.

He leaned closer to the microphone. "Bubbles," he whispered.

I thought maybe I'd heard him wrong.

He said he saw bubbles flying around my spacesuit in the footage of my spacewalk, and that these bubbles were definitive proof that my spacewalk had somehow been faked in a water tank.

I tried to explain. I told him that the tiny flecks he saw floating in space might have been paint chips—the outside of the space station has been blasted by the sun and micrometeorites for the last twenty years, and bits of insulation break loose and float away all the time while we're working.

But that made him angry. "No," he shouted. "Those are bubbles. You were in a swimming pool. This is all fake."

Later, my wife, Amiko, told me she recognized him. He'd shown up at other events to confront astronauts about bubbles or reflections they couldn't explain in a video shot or phantom "wires" supposedly holding us up in the space station because they don't believe we are held aloft in microgravity.

Some people believe that all human spaceflight has been faked, which would require me to have spent twenty years of my life performing on secret NASA soundstages and lying my ass off. To which I reply, if we faked the Moon landing, why haven't we faked going to Mars?

The flat Earthers and Moon-landing truthers dedicate themselves to studying footage from spaceflights looking for "evidence" that the images are faked. But I don't really know what to say to someone who calls me a liar to my face. And not only me—but everyone who has risked their life flying in space or working for the space program to try to advance human knowledge.

They're calling Neil Armstrong a liar, John Glenn a liar. To them, the crew that died in the *Challenger* explosion—which the entire nation witnessed in real time—and my friends who died on *Columbia* are liars.

Social media has clearly played a role in the rise of these anti-science conspiracy theories. When you get all your information from an open forum where any crackpot can post anything they want, it's bound to create confusion and paranoia. Small comments can be blown out of proportion, and jokes can be mistaken for truth.

Twenty years ago, if you believed the conspiracy theory that vaccines were created by tech billionaire Bill Gates to implant microchips to control people, you would only be able to share that ridiculous opinion with your family and friends (who might encourage you to seek mental health treatment). But today, you can blast that opinion out to millions of people on multiple platforms, and it can be harder and harder to tell which voices are credible and which are not.

Not long ago, basketball superstar Steph Curry said

on a podcast that he believed the Moon landings had been faked. To be fair to Steph, another person on the podcast made the claim and Steph just chimed in to agree . . . but that was all it took to set off thousands of tweets, retweets, likes, comments, and media coverage about how Steph was a Moon-landing conspiracist.

I had always thought Steph seemed like a smart guy, and given the context, I felt pretty sure he was just messing around and didn't actually mean to promote this theory. So I reached out to him on Twitter and invited him to discuss the Moon landings with me.

We wound up doing an Instagram Live talk about the whole incident. I shared with him some of the facts I bring up when people express skepticism about the Moon landings:

- The Apollo project employed more than 400,000 people at its peak. The idea that so many people could keep a secret that big for decades is pretty implausible.
- Every successful Moon landing brought back Moon rocks—hundreds of pounds of

them all together. Those rocks were shared with scientists all over the world, including scientists in the Soviet Union, who very much hoped to see us fail. Scientific analysis of the rocks has shown they could only have come from the Moon, and no one has ever disputed their authenticity, even our enemies.

- You can still see all the stuff astronauts left on the Moon through satellite imaging.

Steph was interested in learning these details, and he even came out to the Johnson Space Center to see some of the Moon rocks for himself.

I have a lot of respect for him taking the time to accept responsibility for spreading false conspiracies and then using his platform to clear things up and spread facts instead. People are more likely to believe a claim that's made by someone they look up to and respect, and a lot of people look up to Steph Curry.

I believe it's up to all of us to nip this kind of disinformation in the bud, wherever we find it. If you start to believe one conspiracy theory—that the government lied to us about going to the Moon—you are more likely to believe others, like the government planned 9/11, or that climate change isn't real. It's a dangerous phenomenon, and it's not an exaggeration to say that it can lead to the downfall of a civilization.

Science has given us so much—it's the bedrock of modern human existence. Consider the wheel. Invented in 3,500 BC, it was so complex for its time that it took modern humans nearly 200,000 years to figure it out. Some of the scientific discoveries considered the greatest of all time are fairly recent, like genome editing, RNA sequencing, electricity, and antibiotics. Without science we would still be living in the Stone Age.

Science is based on theories that can either be proven or disproven by research and results that can be repeated and confirmed by others. It's not an opinion that is up for debate or won in a tweetstorm. We all need to insist that facts matter. And remember, it's not always rocket science—but when it is, ask a rocket scientist, not a self-proclaimed expert or your Facebook friend.

Eagle's successful Moon landing during the Apollo 11 mission was the culmination of years of work by thousands of engineers solving problem after problem.

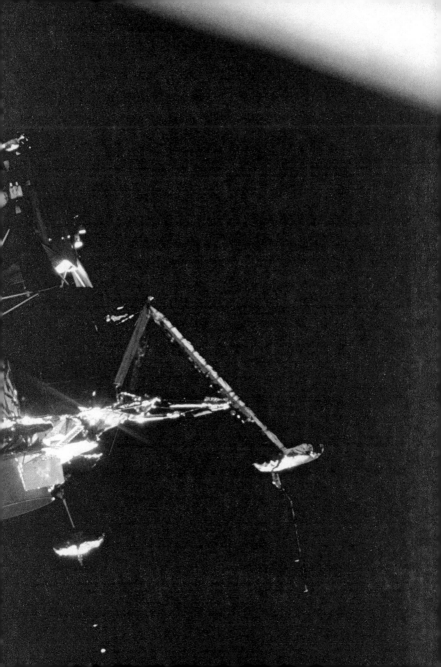

9

TEAMWORK MAKES THE DREAM WORK

Spaceflight is the biggest team sport there is. At least that's what I call it. It's not a sport in the traditional sense, but it does have some shared characteristics; historically, it's been competitive, as evidenced by the Moon race between the United States and the Soviet Union. At times, it's competitive between individuals as well, with astronauts and cosmonauts vying for a coveted flight assignment. It's extremely physical during training, launch, landing, and of course the arduous spacewalks—the most challenging thing I've ever done. And it's highly organized. Putting a space shuttle or other spacecraft into orbit takes thousands of individuals in a myriad of disciplines, from the engineers who design it and the technicians who manufacture and prepare the vehicles for launch to the instructors, flight controllers, and medical and rescue personnel. It is a massive team effort. And those of us on the playing field—the astronauts and cosmonauts—are literally relying on all these folks for our lives.

When I was first assigned to the one-year mission with Misha (Mikhail) Kornienko, in 2013, we didn't know each other well even though we first met around 1999. But neither of us was very good at the other's language, so it was really hard to become friends. As soon as we were assigned to this flight, Misha made sure that I knew we were in it together. Thirteen other people would come and go throughout the year we were aboard ISS, but day in and day out, from March 2015 to March 2016, it would be just Misha and me for the long term. He started to call me "brother" and later, "space brother," once we were on orbit. From a Westerner's perspective, Russians can seem cold and aloof, but once you get to know them you can build stronger friendships quicker than in Western culture. I know this is a generalization, but it also reflects my own personal experience. And the idea of teamwork is emphasized in their space program so much that the cosmonauts as a group are called the "Team of Cosmonauts," whereas at NASA we refer to ourselves as "the Astronaut Office."

When our Soyuz first docked with the ISS, Misha and I were in the habitation module with cosmonaut Gennady Padalka getting ready to open the hatch. Gennady, the Soyuz commander, said to me, "Scott, you float through the hatch first." Normally, either the commander or a first-time flyer, a rookie, will be the first crew member to enter the ISS—though that decision is up to the commander. I was neither commander nor rookie, so Gennady was just being deferential to the only American on the crew. I turned to Misha and said, "Let's float through the hatch together; we're in this as a team." Having a shared goal and set of experiences bonds people. It gives them someone to turn to for advice, companionship, and help getting through the grind of a challenging experience. This is what I had with Misha. He knew what I was going through and vice versa. We could lean on each other for support, which made our performance better.

* * *

Misha wasn't the only one I could lean on during that mission. When I had the opportunity to do my first of three spacewalks nearly seven months into my year in space, it took the dedication of both the ISS and ground crews to complete the assigned task. This was my first spacewalk ever, which you might find unusual for someone who has had such a long and diverse spaceflight career. The reason it was my first was because spacewalks were considered too risky for shuttle pilots and commanders, who were essential for flying the shuttle back to Earth safely. We used to joke that the mission specialists were expendable. Then on my third mission, my first long-duration flight on the ISS, the US crew members just had no reason to do any.

In movies, a spacewalk is often portrayed as a spontaneous event akin to putting on a suit and just stepping outside. But in reality, it's a complex effort that requires weeks of study and air-to-ground conferences, and preparation of the suits, tools, and hardware you might be using or installing on the outside of the ISS. The number of people involved is astounding, all working together like a well-oiled machine. The night before you go outside, you feel like you are anticipating the Super Bowl or some other championship event. Everything needs to be perfect, or you won't be making it back inside.

My second spacewalk was probably the most challenging day of my life. As I floated out of the ISS and into the vacuum of space, Kjell Lindgren, my spacewalking partner, was way out on the truss—the aluminum backbone of the station that supports the solar arrays. The work site was too far out for our tethers to reach, so we used a technique called a daisy chain. Kjell ventured out as far as he could go, then attached my tether while I was still in the air lock. Once I was attached, I followed him, and from this new anchor point we took turns being the one anchored and the one traveling farther out, kind of like an inchworm. We made our way to the end of the truss, which felt really far from the safety of the air lock. Maneuvering yourself in several hundred pounds of spacesuit is both a surreal and arduous process. Being in microgravity means the suit doesn't feel that heavy, but it is still big and bulky, with several hundred pounds of mass, so it takes great effort to control. You are also keenly aware that you are in a cold and airless vacuum while zooming around the planet at incredible speeds. But at least in the beginning of this spacewalk I still had the sense that I was supported by the incredible team on the ground.

In the absence of gravity, your sense of up and down is somewhat arbitrary depending on your surroundings. When I first came out of the air lock, I felt like I was crawling on the floor. The sun was out and I could feel the intense heat through the suit's gloves as I gripped the handrails. Once I got onto the truss, my reference frame shifted, and I felt like I was hanging on to a wall with Earth 250 miles below my feet.

The vivid hues and light are absolutely astonishing when you aren't looking through the filter of our atmosphere. Perfect clarity. I gazed downward as we crossed over the Pacific Ocean. The color was so intense it felt like someone had painted the most brilliant blue imaginable on a mirror right in front of my eyes. But every minute counts during a spacewalk, so I had to focus on the task at hand and keep moving. When I reached Kjell, we set up our work site to repair the external cooling system. Our helmets were practically touching, and we occasionally exchanged looks of astonishment that conveyed, "Can you believe we are actually doing this?"

The job was tough and technically complicated. Working on these incredibly stiff fluid lines and connectors was extremely physical and required intense coordination with the ground control team. Halfway through our work, the CAPCOM came up on the space-to-ground channel to warn us that the venting ammonia could soon lead to a loss of control and communication with the ground. It was at that moment that I realized, despite all the people on the ground who were supporting our spaceflight and even the four crew members inside the space station, the only person I could truly rely on was my spacewalking teammate, Kjell. Luckily, we didn't end up losing attitude control or contact with the ground. But the grueling tasks we had to perform and the isolation we felt gave me a deeper appreciation for the support of my crewmate and the meaning of teamwork.

Teams are dynamic and changing. When you're young, your team might include your parents or guardians and siblings. When you're in school, you might be on a sports team or part of a group project. As you get older, you'll likely work in teams at your job. During the coronavirus pandemic, our teams are clearly those we are quarantined with or those in our pods. It's important to know the abilities of your teammates to help each other and elevate one another, but also to understand that we are all different.

There were things my crewmates were good at that I would never be able to match and likewise things I was better at. But what was most important was that together, we were strong enough to accomplish so much more than we could have done individually. It took 232 spacewalks by astronauts and cosmonauts from nine different countries to build and operate the space station over the last twenty-two years. I am awestruck that we have accomplished this feat without the loss of life or serious injury to a crew member. Teamwork really does make the dream work.

Misha Kornienko and I came through the Soyuz hatch together to start our year in space on the International Space Station as teammates.

10

THERE'S NO CRYING IN SPACE

The phrase "what doesn't kill you makes you stronger" has defined my career. Choosing to do the hard jobs, dealing with adversity, and never, ever giving up have been the secret to my success.

A couple of months after my return from STS-118, a space shuttle mission to the International Space Station, I was in Washington, DC, having dinner with my brother Mark's then fiancée, Congresswoman Gabrielle Giffords, when I got the call that all astronauts long for—the off-hours surprise call from the chief of the Astronaut Office. When I realized who was calling, I immediately anticipated great news about an assignment as a space shuttle commander on my second mission! Instead,

Steve Lindsey, the chief astronaut, said, "Scott, I'd like to assign you to a long-duration spaceflight, Expedition 25 and 26. You would be the commander of Expedition 26."

I felt immediately deflated. I saw myself more as a space shuttle pilot/commander type. After all, I had been a military test pilot, and there were very few shuttle missions left to be assigned before the shuttle program ended. And I knew that spending six months in space on the ISS is not easy, so my instinctive reaction was to push back. Instead, I thanked Steve for the call and told him I would think it over.

This was a mission I needed to give some serious thought to, especially since I had young kids at the time. It wasn't a decision I took lightly. But, like many things I've been asked to do throughout my career that were hard or disappointing, I ultimately said I would do it.

I've found that my preferred assignments did not always align with the priorities of those in charge. In the US Navy, I was assigned to be an F-14 Tomcat pilot when I really wanted to fly the newer and more advanced F/A-18 Hornet. But landing the Tomcat on a carrier ship at night is probably the most challenging piloting task of all and much harder than landing the F/A-18. My earlier career disappointments not only taught me how to deal with failure when I disqualified on my first attempt to land the Tomcat on the aircraft carrier, but they made me a much better fighter pilot. And that ultimately helped me become an astronaut.

After my first shuttle flight I was asked to live in Russia for nine months as the director of operations in Star City, when I really wanted to be an ascent entry CAPCOM, the astronaut who works in Mission Control as a critical part of the flight control team. Because I agreed to work in Russia, the Astronaut Office decided they could also count on me to accept an assignment as a backup ISS crew member when my nine months were up—another job I didn't want. In the early days of the ISS program, the chief astronaut had a hard time finding crew members to serve as long-duration astronauts aboard the ISS, especially as the backup crew. But because I said yes to this less desirable assignment, I was finally rewarded with the command of a space shuttle mission on just my second flight into space, which was very uncommon.

Beyond disappointing job assignments, I faced the ultimate challenge when I received a cancer diagnosis after my second shuttle mission. As a NASA astronaut, I have been looked after by an incredibly dedicated and talented medical team from the time I interviewed in 1995 at the age of thirty-one until today. I've been poked, prodded, and monitored extensively, and it saved my life by catching my cancer at a very early stage. But hearing the words "you have cancer" is not something for which you are ever truly prepared. I tried to maintain a positive attitude and to approach this with the same level of focus and attention to detail as a fighter pilot, test pilot, and astronaut.

I had a great team of doctors and an advocate in my new flight surgeon, Dr. Steve Gilmore. My treatment plan included prostate surgery in November 2007, and by January, I was back flying jet airplanes. Recovering from prostate surgery isn't easy, but a few months later I was doing my first spacewalk training runs in NASA's Neutral Buoyancy Laboratory. In March 2010, about two and a half years after surgery, I was launching into space on my third spaceflight.

There were a lot of obstacles to getting medically certified for flight after this type of cancer treatment. I'm only aware of one other person who had flown in space after having prostate surgery, and that was my crewmate Dave Williams from STS-118. My situation was different from Dave's because my next mission would be a long-duration flight on the ISS, not a shuttle flight. And I would need to have Russian approval since I would be launching on their Soyuz to get to the ISS. In Russia, the techniques for prostate cancer surgery weren't as advanced and the outcomes weren't as good as they were in the United States, so this was going to be an uphill climb. But with the help of my friend Dr. Steve Gilmore, we were able to get the Russians to reluctantly agree.

It would have been easy to give up when I was diagnosed with cancer, but I didn't—and I went on to fly an additional 500 days in space as a cancer survivor, including my yearlong mission. We don't have to like hardships to accept them. But I have found that we can learn the most from their discomfort.

Adversity changes us, for better or for worse. How adversity shapes us depends on how we choose to respond to it. We all have challenges—doing poorly on a test, getting cut from a sports team, or losing a job—but when we meet them head-on, we develop critical skills like grit and perseverance that prepare us for the next hard moment in life. Overcoming adversity draws out our true strengths and gives us the opportunity to believe in ourselves.

We don't succeed in spite of our challenges; we succeed because of them.

When I took off for my Year in Space, I was prepared to face any challenge with the help of my two crewmates, Misha (top) and Gennady (bottom).

FINAL THOUGHTS

––––––

In outer space, 254 miles up, above everything you know and love and have seen in your lifetime, the ISS is orbiting our planet sixteen times every day. You can actually see it yourself every now and then, when it passes overhead around dawn or dusk. And when you do, the ISS is a powerful reminder that Space belongs to all of us, and its exploration is a shared human endeavor—one I'm proud to be a part of.

I've been fascinated by this challenge since I was eighteen years old and first picked up that copy of *The Right Stuff*. For a long time, though, I wasn't sure if that book would be the closest I would get to experiencing spaceflight myself. To be honest, if I hadn't found that book, I know I wouldn't have made it as far as I did. Eighteen years after I first read it, I was flying into space for the first time.

The power of inspiration cannot be measured by the deeds of the uninspired but by the achievements of children as they realize their dreams. I was one of those kids.

I want to make sure I leave you with a few final thoughts. Our capacity for learning and growing is infinite. And if you are prepared to learn from every lesson, every failure, and every person you meet along the way, nothing can stop you. You can realize your dreams if you reach for the stars.

Sure, you'll make mistakes, you'll fail, you'll be afraid sometimes, but you'll see how leading with strength, using empathy, embracing diversity, and listening to others will mold you into the successful person you can be. Only by taking the biggest risks can you reach the biggest rewards.

When we put in the work, lean into science and truth, and allow ourselves the honesty of learning from our mistakes, we are amazing creatures who can literally discover new worlds and solve the problems before us. If we can dream it, we can do it.

You might be dreaming of a life in space; you might be dreaming of a life here on Earth. We all have unique aspirations. The astronauts who are stationed on the ISS right now may be looking down, dreaming of things in your life—the smell of grass, a cold plunge into a lake, or the feeling of a soft, warm bed. And who knows? A kid who could be sitting on the launchpad someday might be looking back up at them right now, dreaming of their life and starting to make a plan to do the impossible.

Lying on my back getting ready to launch on my first ride into space on *Discovery* was the moment that my astronaut dream took flight.

ACKNOWLEDGMENTS

———

I'd like to thank my wife, Amiko, for her help making this book—and our life together—better. Of course, my collaborator, Emily Easton, was critical to this effort. I would also like to thank my friend Margaret Lazarus Dean and her sister, Sarah Lazarus, for their help with this book. But I'd especially like to thank all my former colleagues, crewmates, teammates, instructors, leaders, friends, and family who shaped me into the person I am today and helped me get ready for launch.

ABOUT THE AUTHOR

Scott Kelly is a retired NASA astronaut best known for spending a record-breaking year in space. He is a former US Navy fighter pilot, test pilot, and veteran of four spaceflights. Kelly commanded the space shuttle *Endeavour* in 2007 and commanded the International Space Station three times on two flights. He lives in Littleton, Colorado. You can follow him on Facebook at NASA Astronaut Scott Kelly, and on Instagram and Twitter at @StationCDRKelly.

scottkelly.com